98

INVENTORS

INVENTORS

A LIBRARY OF CONGRESS BOOK

BY MARTIN W. SANDLER

Introduction by James H. Billington, Librarian of Congress

HarperCollins*Publishers*

For Laura, Jill, Susan, Scott and Craig

ACKNOWLEDGMENTS

The author wishes to thank John Cole and Peggy Wagner of the Publishing Office of the Library of Congress for their help and support. Appreciation is expressed also to Liza Baker, Craig D'Oogie, the staff of the Prints and Photographs Division of the Library of Congress and Dennis Magnu of the Library's Photoduplication Service. As with all the books in this series, this volume and its author owe much to the guidance and editorial skill of Kate Morgan Jackson.

◆

Inventors
A Library of Congress Book
Copyright © 1996 by Eagle Productions, Inc.

For information address HarperCollins Children's Books, a division of HarperCollins Publishers,
10 East 53rd Street, New York, NY 10022.

Library of Congress Cataloging-in-Publication Data
Sandler, Martin W.
Inventors / by Martin W. Sandler ; introduction by James H. Billington.
p.   cm.
"A Library of Congress Book"
ISBN 0-06-024923-4. — ISBN 0-06-024924-2 (lib. bdg.)
1. Inventions—United States—History—19th century—Juvenile literature.   2. Inventions—United States—History—20th century—Juvenile literature.   3. Inventions—United States—History—19th century—Pictorial works—Juvenile literature.   4. Inventions—United States—History—20th century—Pictorial works—Juvenile literature.
5. Inventors—United States—History—19th century—Juvenile literature.   6. Inventors—United States—History—20th century—Juvenile literature.   [1. Inventions—History.   2. Inventors—History.]   I. Title.
T21.S28   1996
609.2´273—dc20
95-944
CIP
AC

Design by Tom Starace with Cliff Bachner
1   2   3   4   5   6   7   8   9   10
❖
First Edition

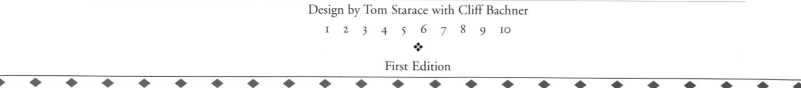

Our type of democracy has depended upon and grown with knowledge gained through books and all the other various records of human memory and imagination. By their very nature, these records foster freedom and dignity. Historically they have been the companions of a responsible, democratic citizenry. They provide keys to the dynamism of our past and perhaps to our national competitiveness in the future. They link the record of yesterday with the possibilities of tomorrow.

One of our main purposes at the Library of Congress is to make the riches of the Library even more available to even wider circles of our multiethnic society. Thus we are proud to lend our name and resources to this series of children's books. We share Martin W. Sandler's goal of enriching our greatest natural resource—the minds and imaginations of our young people.

The scope and variety of Library of Congress print and visual materials contained in these books demonstrate that libraries are the starting places for the adventure of learning that can go on whatever one's vocation and location in life. They demonstrate that reading is an adventure like the one that is discovery itself. Being an American is not a patent of privilege but an invitation to adventure. We must go on discovering America.

James H. Billington
The Librarian of Congress

From the days of Benjamin Franklin, well before the United States became an independent nation, Americans have been characterized by their inventive spirit. This genius for innovation has profoundly changed the way people around the world work, play, move about, communicate and are entertained. In the process the men and women responsible for many of these advancements have joined the ranks of the nation's greatest heroes. In the pages that follow, you will meet these innovators and will discover how their inventions affect your own life every day.

MARTIN W. SANDLER

AN INVENTIVE SPIRIT

As the year 1876 begins, the United States prepares to celebrate its one hundredth birthday. It is a time of rejoicing and great optimism. "The last hundred years," writes the *New York Herald*, "have been the most fruitful and the most glorious period of equal length in the history of the human race."

There is indeed much of which to be proud. The United States has not only established itself as a great nation, it has demonstrated an inventive spirit unlike any the world has ever known.

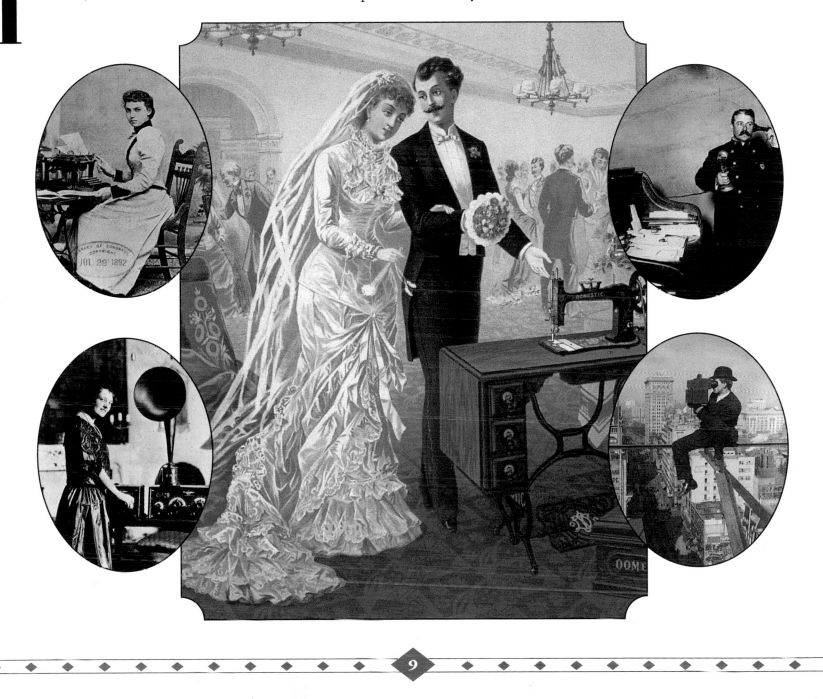

The United States is about to enter a magical time in history. Thanks to new inventions, the darkness of night will be set aglow. People in all corners of the nation will be given the means to talk to one another. House, farm and office tasks will become more efficient and less burdensome than ever before.

Before the twentieth century begins, products and devices created in the United States will improve ways of life throughout the world. A nation so proud of its statesmen and military figures will discover a brand-new type of hero—the American inventor.

The only Route via NIAGARA FALLS & SUSPENSION BRIDGE

I ncluded in the extraordinary array of inventions will be machines and devices that will change the way people move about. New modes of transportation will make traveling long distances easier than was ever thought possible.

"Where do all these inventors come from?" a foreign observer wonders. "They have conquered the land and reached for the sky. Is there nothing they will not seek to change?"

PRODUCTS OF INVENTION

One of the first and most important devices developed in what will later be called the "great age of American invention" is the telegraph. It is created by Samuel F. B. Morse, who begins work on his invention in the 1830's and receives a patent for it in 1844. The telegraph allows messages to be sent via pulses of electricity carried from one terminal to another over wires. Morse makes his invention practical for even the youngest users by also inventing a system known as Morse code that permits a person to send a telegraphic message by tapping out a series of clicks with pauses in between on a simple transmitting key.

Above: Samuel F. B. Morse
Right: Young boy receiving a message by telegraph

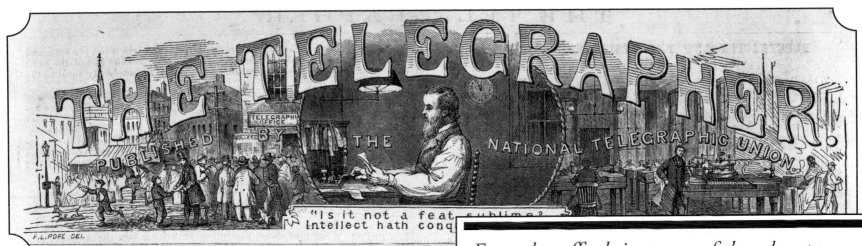

THE TELEGRAPHER!

PUBLISHED BY THE NATIONAL TELEGRAPHIC UNION.

"Is it not a feat sublime?
Intellect hath conq...

F.L.POPE DEL.

The telegraph marks the beginning of a communications revolution. Newspapers throughout the nation use the word *telegraph* in their titles to emphasize their speedier access to events. During the Civil War both armies erect hundreds of telegraph poles and string miles of wire to enable troops to keep in touch as never before. By 1883 the Western Union Company, founded by Morse and his partner, Alfred Vail, transmits millions of messages annually over more than 400,000 miles of wire strung throughout the nation. The telegraph hastens the development of a national railroad system and has a vital impact on almost every aspect of American life.

"The American invents as the Italian paints and the Greek sculpted. It is genius," a foreign visitor to the United States exclaims. While the telegraph becomes known worldwide, work is being carried out on scores of other inventions, including the rotary press, the typewriter, the vulcanization of rubber and dozens of farm implements.

In 1846 a major breakthrough takes place when Elias Howe introduces the world's first sewing machine, an invention destined to make the age-old task of sewing easier for people everywhere.

Some five years after Elias Howe introduces his sewing machine, Isaac Singer receives a patent for a slightly different model. Singer is one of the first inventors to understand the importance of aggressively advertising a product. He introduces new sales techniques, such as allowing customers to purchase his machine through time payments. Singer also realizes the enormous potential for foreign sales. Soon advertisements for his product appear in nations throughout the world.

When woman toiled for daily bread from early morn to eve,
How many eyes were dimmed with tears; how many hearts did grieve.
But now she has her "household pet" and one to which she'll cling,
For labor is a pleasure now, and she can toil and sing. . . .

—Untitled poem celebrating the sewing machine, c. 1855, author unknown

The sewing machine is a true labor-saving device, and soon there is another product that will have great impact, particularly for countless office workers. Since the early 1700's inventors around the world have been attempting to create a practical writing machine. Success is finally achieved in the late 1860's by Christopher Sholes, a Milwaukee newspaper publisher and politician turned inventor. Working sixteen hours a day for more than ten years, Sholes eventually solves the jamming problem that has plagued all previous models by having the carriage on his machine move one space to the left when a letter is typed.

Christopher Sholes, along with fellow inventor Carlos Glidden and their financial backer, James Densmore, receives a patent for the typewriter in 1868. Densmore then sells the manufacturing and distributing rights to the machine to E. Remington and Sons, one of the nation's largest makers of firearms. By the mid-1880's the Remington typewriter is found in most American offices. The most popular courses in the nation's business schools become those that teach the new skill called typing.

Whatever I may have thought in the early days of the value of the typewriter, it is very obviously a blessing to mankind, and especially to womankind. I am very glad I had something to do with it. I builded wiser than I knew, and the world has the benefit of it.

—Christopher Sholes, c. 1875

WORLD'S GREATEST INVENTOR

Thomas Edison with dictaphone

In the same year that Christopher Sholes and his colleagues receive a patent for the typewriter, the man who will become the greatest inventor the world has ever known bursts upon the scene. Thomas Alva Edison is only twenty-one when, in 1868, he receives his first patent, for an electrical vote recorder. Before he is thirty, he develops an astounding array of devices, including the mimeograph, the dictaphone, improvements on the telegraph, and one of the most important of all his inventions, the phonograph. All told, Edison patents more than a thousand inventions leading to the emergence of more than a dozen new industries.

Right: Thomas Edison

W̲ith the money he makes from his early inventions, Edison establishes an "invention factory" at Menlo Park, New Jersey. Known as "The Wizard of Menlo Park," Edison, along with the other inventors and mechanics he hires, produces an average of one patentable device every two weeks. These devices include inventions that will help in the development of the telephone, the radio and television. Among them, too, is a motion-picture projector that paves the way for the beginnings of America's giant movie industry.

10TH ON COURT HOUSE SQUARE
PHOTO BY GAS LIGHT   SCRANTON PA.
COPYRIGHT 1911
HORGAN OF SCRANTON

dison's list of accomplishments is remarkable, but it is the electric light bulb that brings him his greatest fame and transforms ways of living like no other innovation. Since the days of Benjamin Franklin's experiments with electricity, American inventors had been attempting to produce artificial light by passing electricity through a thin filament in a vacuum tube. In 1877 Edison and his Menlo Park assistants begin work on this challenging project. Late in 1879 they hit upon a carbonized filament that glows brightly in a vacuum tube for up to forty hours.

etween 1879 and 1882 Edison invents screw-in sockets, light switches, meters and improved dynamos, along with other items needed for a system capable of delivering electricity to the nation.

Left: Coney Island amusement park at night

In 1882 the Edison Illuminating Company opens a power station in New York. By 1898 more than 3,600 such facilities are supplying electricity throughout America. By 1905 entire cities have lighting capacity. Patterns of work and play are changed forever.

HOTHOUSE OF ACTIVITY

SELF-PROPELLING ICE SLEIGHS

The successes achieved by Morse, Sholes, Singer, Edison and other innovators turn America into an even greater hothouse of inventive activity. Garages and basements are converted into workshops and primitive laboratories, where every type of contraption imaginable is conceived. Between 1860 and 1890 the U.S. Patent Office grants almost 450,000 patent applications for devices ranging from a self-propelled hobbyhorse to a treadmill with which farm animals generate electricity while housed in their stalls.

Many of these ideas, including one for making swimming easier and another for a trolley car in the shape of a horse (to avoid frightening real horses), are never developed beyond the blueprint stage. But they all add to the ever-increasing notion that with the right new twist, the right tools and some luck, almost anyone can invent something that will bring fame and riches.

M ost of the newly proposed contraptions never make it into the marketplace. Other proposed devices, though unsuccessful in their day, are far ahead of their time. One such idea is for a flying machine with a vertical liftoff, a feature that will become the distinguishing characteristic of modern-day helicopters. In the 1870's a device called the pedespeed is ridiculed, but it is not that far removed from today's in-line skates.

Invention breeds invention.

—Author Ralph Waldo Emerson, in one of his letters, 1870

Leslie's

Illustrated Weekly Newspaper
Established in 1855

PRICE 10 CENTS

The Party Wire

By the time the nation celebrates its hundredth birthday, in 1876, a host of American inventors have made their mark. At the giant Centennial Exposition in Philadelphia, more than 12,000 awards are given out to innovators such as Cyrus McCormick, inventor of the mechanical reaper; Elisha Otis, inventor of the elevator; and George Westinghouse, developer of the air brake. One of the most popular individuals at the exposition is an inventor named Alexander Graham Bell, who introduces a new device that he calls the telephone.

Alexander Graham Bell

[W]herever you may find the inventor, you may give him wealth or you may take from him all that he has; and he will go on inventing.

—Alexander Graham Bell, c. 1880

Bell's invention of the telephone stems from his conviction that with the right transmitter in place, sound could be carried over wires by a continuous electrical current varying in intensity. In June 1875, after years of experimentation, Bell and his assistant, Thomas A. Watson, come up with a transmitter that works.

The telephone is an immediate sensation, a giant step beyond the telegraph, in that it transmits speech. More importantly, whereas the telegraph provides communication from one telegraph office to another, the telephone allows people to talk to each other in their own homes and businesses. By 1900 there are 1,365,000 telephones in use across the nation. Ten years later, the number rises to 7.6 million.

The telephone will become so popular that between 1876 and 1976, well over 3 million men and women will find employment as telephone operators, installers and repairers.

Eventually, telephone wires in many cities are buried underground, but well into the twentieth century they provide visible testimony to one of the world's greatest inventions.

L ike Edison, Alexander Graham Bell will be responsible for scores of inventions, including the iron lung, the hydrofoil, disc phonograph records, land-mine detectors and underwater sounding devices. He will conduct many aeronautical experiments and will produce innovations that contribute to the development of the airplane. The telephone, however, will remain his best-known invention and will change American life more than any of his other inventions.

Alexander Graham Bell and assistants experiment with multicell kite

He makes you feel that if only you had a little more time, you, too, might be an inventor.

—Helen Keller, upon first meeting Alexander Graham Bell, c. 1875

The inventors and scientists who leave their mark on America come from every segment of the nation's population. A number of these innovators are African Americans. In the 1870's Elijah McCoy perfects a device for lubricating machinery that improves manufacturing efficiency around the world. In the 1880's Jan E. Metzeliger develops a machine for mass-producing shoes that revolutionizes that industry. The roster of African-American inventors comes to include Lewis N. Latimer, who introduces one of the world's first incandescent lamps; Granville T. Woods, who produces a score of inventions that improve electric railways; and A. J. Beard, who in 1897 introduces an improved car coupler that makes railroad travel safer and more efficient. The world of medicine benefits enormously from the innovations of Dr. Daniel Hale Williams, who in 1893 performs the first human-heart operation, and Dr. Charles R. Drew, who revolutionizes the medical profession by inventing a method of extracting and transfusing blood plasma.

The most renowned of all African-American inventors and scientists is George Washington Carver, who revitalizes agriculture in the South by proving that the planting of peanuts can replenish worn-out soil. Carver then introduces scores of important products that can be made from the peanut crop. Carver, second from the right in this photograph, is also credited with performing another vital service: spending long hours working with African-American students and introducing them to the world of science and invention.

George Washington Carver in laboratory

THE WONDER OF STEEL

A s the last quarter of the 1800's begins, the pace of American inventions gains even greater momentum. Many of the inventions that fol- low are made possible by a development in the steelmaking process, pioneered in England by Henry Bessemer and in America by William Kelly. Steel allows for the building of a variety of machines that come to dominate the American landscape.

COMBINED HARVESTER & THRASHER   NO 1054
PHOTO BY

By the 1880's America is the largest producer of steel and machinery in the world. Many of the machines are designed to make life easier and more productive for farmers, who comprise the largest group of workers in the nation. Thanks to new machinery, these farmers, particularly those on the vast American prairie, are turning the United States into an agricultural giant.

New and efficient methods of manufacturing steel change the face of the city as well. The strongest building material of the day, steel allows for the construction of skyscrapers, buildings that reach as many as twenty stories high. They are marvels of their time, made possible not only by steel but by yet another invention, the elevator, which provides easy transport to even the highest floors.

Flatiron Building, New York City

American cities come to be characterized not only by skyscrapers but by enormous steel bridges. The first of these great bridges is the multispan St. Louis Bridge, which crosses the Mississippi River. One of the most spectacular is the 1,595-foot Brooklyn Bridge in New York, which takes fourteen years to complete. More than twenty men, including the project's initiator, John Roebling, die during its construction; but finally, on May 24, 1883, the magnificent structure officially opens.

Celebration of the opening of the Brooklyn Bridge

In things of iron and steel . . .
the national genius most freely speaks.
—Novelist William Dean Howells, c. 1876

As the 1800's draw to a close, inventions have made life less burdensome for millions of people. Americans, who have always been characterized by hard work, begin to find more time to play. Throughout the nation, enterprising businessmen build giant playgrounds called amusement parks and fill them with inventions designed to bring pleasure and thrills.

The progress brought to life by this inventive spirit is celebrated in world's fairs and expositions held throughout the nation. Along with displays of new machines and new devices, these fairs and expositions also introduce new marvels of amusement. The most spectacular of all is unveiled at Chicago's Columbian Exposition, in 1893. It is George Ferris's giant revolving wheel, standing 264 feet high and holding 60 passengers in each of its 36 cars.

Our inventors are leading us to new worlds of play. Everything . . . is changing in a dizzying whirl.

—Kansas newspaperman, 1896

CAPTURED MOMENTS

The inventions keep on coming. Between 1875 and 1900 the web printing press, the Linotype machine, the adding machine, the fountain pen, the safety razor, the electric welding machine and many other devices are all introduced. These advances are recorded by another miracle of the age: the camera.

From that moment onward . . . society rushed . . . to contemplate its image on a metallic plate.

—French poet Charles Baudelaire, 1859, speaking of the birth of photography

The first form of photography is called the daguerreotype, named after the Frenchman Louis Daguerre, who in 1839 successfully captures a permanent photographic image. Although the daguerreotype is a one-of-a-kind positive image that cannot be reproduced, it causes a sensation. It's an enormous hit in America, where people from all walks of life experience the ordeal of sitting motionless before the camera for up to twenty minutes to have their likenesses preserved. Within twelve years the daguerreotype is made obsolete by other forms of photography.

In 1851 Englishman Frederick Scott Archer introduces an important new photographic process whereby glass plates record negative images, from which countless prints can be made. Coated with a jellylike substance called collodion, these "wet plates" must be developed almost immediately. The process is embraced in America, where early photographers haul bulky cameras and huge glass plates into the field, hoping to capture spectacular scenes of the unsettled West and, from 1861 to 1865, horrific images of a bitter Civil War.

Photographer in Yosemite Valley, California

Civil War soldiers

I cannot . . . describe all the wonders of The Apparatus. Suffice it to say I can now make a <u>perfect</u> picture in one hour's time that would take a Painter weeks to draw.

—Early American photographer, c. 1850

You press the button, we do the rest.

—George Eastman's slogan for his camera company, c. 1890

I n 1880 another important advancement, the "dry plate," is introduced, relieving photographers of the burden of having to develop their negatives immediately. Eight years later one of the most important photographic inventions of all time is put on the market by George Eastman, a dry-plate manufacturer from Rochester, New York. Eastman's invention is a simple hand-held camera that contains another Eastman invention, a roll of flexible film capable of taking 100 pictures. When the roll is completed, the sealed camera is sent to Eastman's factory, where prints are made and a new roll of film is inserted. Eastman gives the name KODAK to his invention. It is a name that has no meaning but one that the inventor believes will be easily remembered by consumers. By the end of the 1880s, the new camera revolutionizes photography by making it accessible to everyone, including the youngest picture takers.

It is one thing to photograph people: It is another thing to make others care about them by revealing the core of their humanness.

—Photographer Paul Strand, c. 1940

hanks to George Eastman and the other inventors who follow him, photography becomes both a billion-dollar industry and the most popular hobby the world has ever known. Photographers, amateur and professional, not only document every aspect of American life but also produce images that capture the full range of human emotions and experiences. Some images, such as Arthur Rothstein's photograph of a father and his sons caught in a 1930's dust storm, become as well known as the most popular paintings.

World War I battle

In the closing years of the 1800's, another photographic invention, the halftone, makes it possible to print photographs in newspapers and magazines. A whole new type of photographer, soon to be called the photojournalist, travels the world to capture images that bring the major events of the day into the homes of readers everywhere.

At the same time, other photographers explore methods of producing pictures that turn even the most common scenes into images of great sensitivity and beauty. Thanks to the photographs they produce and the influence their work will have on future photographers, photography will become not only a powerful means of recording the world but a recognized and honored form of art.

"The Ring Toss" by photographer Clarence White

In 1930 another important photographic advance is made with the introduction of color film by Leopold Mannes and Leopold Godowsky. A few early photographers had hand colored some of their images, and some turn-of-the-century cameramen and camerawomen had employed a special electroplating process to produce color. It is not, however, until 1938, after Mannes and Godowsky's process has been perfected, that color film is made available to photographers everywhere. The use of color brings a whole new dimension to photography, providing yet another example of how, in the world of invention, one important innovation often leads to many others.

It is the mission of art to remind man that he is human.

—Painter and photographer
Ben Shahn, c. 1965

TRAVEL TIME!

"There is not a man here," says a senator from New York, "who does not feel four hundred percent bigger in 1900 [than ever before], bigger intellectually, bigger hopefully, bigger patriotically." It is an optimism fueled by the extraordinary changes that have engulfed the nation. And nowhere are the changes more profound than in the way Americans move about. In the last decades of the 1800's, the spirit of invention produces not only a communications and an industrial revolution but a revolution in transportation as well.

> *What is this steam going to lead to? Till now man has been bound to a single spot like an oyster or a tree. . . . [Steam] is going to alter, in a degree far more remarkable than any previous change, the condition of mankind.*
>
> —New York *Mirror,* c. 1835

Many of America's transportation changes derive from experiments with steam, first conducted in the 1700's. In August of 1807 the harnessing of steam for transportation becomes a reality when Robert Fulton, building on the work of an earlier inventor, John Fitch, navigates his steam-driven vessel, the *Clermont,* 150 miles up the Hudson River from New York City to Albany. Within thirty years America's great rivers will be filled with hundreds of steamboats carrying passengers and goods. By the mid-1800's huge oceangoing steamships will cut in half the one-month journey by sailing vessel from America to Europe.

The steamship dramatically changes the way millions of people travel, but it is a much simpler transportation invention that captures the fancy of the entire nation. Among its many attractions, the Philadelphia Centennial Exposition of 1876 introduces Americans to a newly improved chain-driven two-wheel bicycle. It is the beginning of a love affair that remains with us today.

By the mid-1890's more than 500 American factories are turning out bikes. And in garages and workshops across the nation, mechanics and tinkerers seek fame and fortune by experimenting with new ways to make two-wheeled vehicles faster and more comfortable.

> *We claim a great utility that*
> *   daily must increase;*
> *We claim from inactivity a*
> *   sensible release;*
> *A constant mental, physical*
> *   and moral help we feel,*
> *That bids us turn enthusiasts,*
> *   and cry, "God bless the*
> *   wheel!"*
>
> —Late 1800's poem, author unknown

Almost everyone can learn to ride a bicycle, and almost everyone does. Less than twenty years after its invention, more than 10 million cyclists have taken to the road, including women dressed in specially designed skirts that rise above the ankles to enable easy pedaling. People throughout the nation join bicycling clubs and take part in bicycle tours. By 1900, at the peak of the cycling craze, regularly scheduled bicycle races and tournaments draw more spectators than major-league baseball games.

The bicycle not only provides exercise but allows people to explore the countryside and visit nearby towns. Soon, however, there will be an invention that will make moving about even easier. In the 1870's American cities become filled with horse-drawn trolley cars designed to transport people from neighborhood to neighborhood and from city residences to stores, theaters and restaurants.

In 1888 a major breakthrough is made. A former employee of Thomas Alva Edison's named Frank Sprague begins operating the nation's first electric trolley system in Richmond, Virginia. Within seven years there will be over 10,000 miles of trolley tracks laid in American cities.

012910. LABOR DAY CROWD, MAIN ST. BUFFALO, N.Y.   COPYRIGHT 1900, BY DETROIT PHOTOGRAPHIC CO.

By 1900 the trolley becomes the chief means of urban transportation. It is swift without being dangerous and is the most efficient and comfortable means of travel yet devised.

To the already deafening clamor of our cities, a new sound has been added. The constant, clattering clang of the trolley.

—Milwaukee newspaperman, 1873

Soon there are interconnecting systems that enable passengers to travel huge distances entirely by trolley. As trolley lines reach out into the rural areas surrounding the city, a whole new type of community, the suburb, is created, enabling men and women to toil in the city while living in the fresh air of the countryside. Enterprising trolley owners increase ridership by promoting special sight-seeing excursions as well as entertainments that take place on the trolley itself.

Women, in an age of long skirts and strict codes of etiquette, are challenged to find ways of boarding the new trolley cars. To meet the challenge, high schools conduct classes designed to teach young ladies the proper way to board the vehicles with safety and decorum.

> *Do not forget your personal appearance. Nothing gives a motorman a better stand in the public eye than to be clean and neatly dressed. If there is anything that disgusts me it is to sit behind a motorman and gaze on a neck so dirty that you could raise a crop of potatoes on it.*
>
> —From "Advice to Motormen," published by the Chicago Trolley Company, 1904

articularly in the cities, the trolley will remain a major means of transportation until well into the 1940's. It will be celebrated in song and story, and the nation will embrace a brand-new type of hero—the trolley motorman.

ALL ABOARD

CATSKILL ROUTE
PROMPT CONNECTIONS BOAT RAIL
FOR ALL POINTS NORTH SOUTH
HAINES CORNERS STATION

The steamship, the bicycle and the trolley are marvels of their time, but in an age of unbridled invention there are even greater transportation developments ahead. Within thirty years of Robert Fulton's success with the steamboat, the steam-driven iron locomotive will become the very symbol of American progress.

The development of the railway train begins in America in 1825. An inventor named John Stevens builds a steam-driven locomotive and runs it on a circular track in Hoboken, New Jersey. Four years later a canal engineer, Horatio Allen, successfully drives his steam locomotive, the *Sturbridge Lion*, along a sixteen-mile track in northern Pennsylvania. In 1831 America's first passenger train, the *De Witt Clinton*, makes its initial run between Albany and Schenectady, New York, on the newly formed Mohawk and Hudson Railway. Like others of the earliest trains, the *De Witt Clinton* pulls its passengers along in cars made from stagecoach bodies.

By 1835 there are more than a thousand miles of track in the eastern United States. Thanks to continued improvements in locomotives, the age-old dream of traveling a mile a minute is about to become a reality.

[The train] will upset all the gravity of the nation. . . . Upon the whole, sir, it is a . . . topsy, turvy, harem-scarem whirligig. . . . None of your hop, skip and jump whimsies for me.

—American newspaper reporter, 1830

Progress in the development of locomotives, cars, tracks and other railway equipment is so rapid that by the 1850's an observer will predict that "the time is not far off when the locomotive will be steaming its way to the Rocky Mountains with a mighty big train of cars running after it." By the 1860's his prediction comes true, and by 1869 a transcontinental railway line has been completed, linking the Pacific to the Atlantic.

The train changes American life in almost every way. Towns and cities spring up along its tracks. Goods are shipped in and out of even the most remote areas. The settlement of the vast western territories is hastened by the arrival of hundreds of thousands of pioneers who travel to the prairie lands by train.

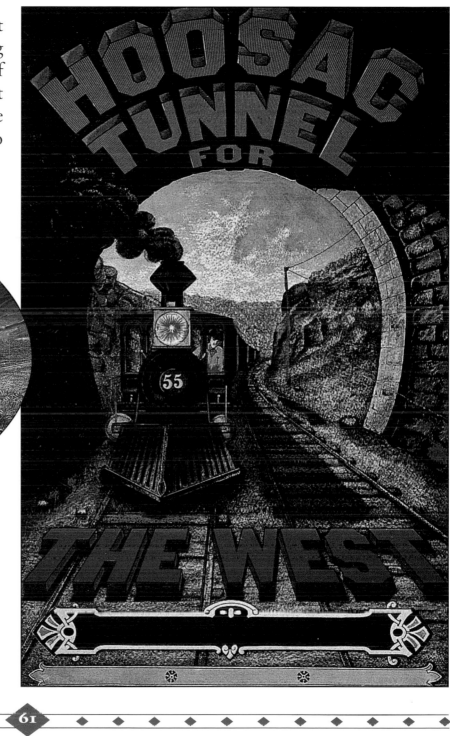

The whistle of the engine will [soon] echo through the South-west Pass, and sharply hint to the free people of that great territory the approach of hundreds and thousands who are to be their neighbors.

—American newspaperman, c. 1850

"We are fast developing into a nation endlessly and anxiously awaiting its trains," writes a nineteenth-century scholar. The railway depot becomes the hub of a community's existence. Throughout America, for passengers and onlookers alike, "watching the trains come in" becomes a favorite pastime.

The changes now taking place have been wrought and are being wrought mainly, almost wholly, by a single mechanical contrivance, the steam locomotive. The railway is the greatest centralizing force of modern times.

—Future president James A. Garfield, 1873

A s the railway system continues to grow, the railroads become the nation's largest employer, providing work for tens of thousands of engineers, conductors, porters, track layers, repairmen, ticket sellers and others. Inventors introduce a host of new devices designed to make train travel safer, including electric headlamps, improved couplings, safety switches and signaling devices. The most important of these inventions is the air brake, developed by George Westinghouse in 1869 when he is only twenty-three years old.

New inventions make railway travel not only safer but far more comfortable. In the late 1860's, George Pullman introduces the sleeping car, making overnight travel more enjoyable. During the same period, luxurious dining cars and coaches are introduced. For millions of Americans, "getting there" by train becomes one of life's great experiences.

By 1898 nearly half the railway mileage in the entire world is found in the United States. Along with millions of passengers, American trains have transported some 800 million tons of goods. With its powerful steam-belching locomotive, its grandiose dining and sleeping cars and its long line of coaches, the train seems to be the ultimate machine. In 1900 there are few who would disagree with the poet Walt Whitman, who characterizes the train as ". . . type of the modern! emblem of motion! pulse of the continent!"

AUTOMOBILES!

Those who are convinced that the train is the ultimate machine have not learned the lessons of the age in which they live, an age that continually turns new ideas into new machines and new devices. And in the early 1900's a whole new type of transportation emerges. Unlike the trolley or the train, it is not tied to tracks. It can go almost anywhere. Those who have taken the bicycle, the trolley and the train to their hearts are about to begin their greatest love affair of all—with the automobile.

AL. JOLSON'S TERRIFIC HIT!

HE'D HAVE TO GET UNDER-
GET OUT AND GET UNDER
(TO FIX UP HIS AUTOMOBILE)

WORDS BY
GRANT CLARKE &
EDGAR LESLIE
MUSIC BY
MAURICE ABRAHAMS

MAURICE ABRAHAMS MUSIC CO

Like so many other inventions, the automobile is the result of the experimentation of countless of tinkerers, mechanics and serious innovators. But it is one man, Henry Ford, who gains the greatest wealth and glory and who is responsible for putting millions of people behind the wheel of an automobile.

Henry Ford and his first car

The automobile that makes Henry Ford both rich and famous is named the Model T. The factory where he first produces this car in 1909 employs a system of mechanical conveyors invented years earlier by Oliver Evans. Another feature of this manufacturing process is the use of mass-produced interchangeable parts, an innovation first developed by the early American inventor Eli Whitney. Ford's assembly-line production system enables him to produce more automobiles in 1914 than all his competitors combined. By 1927 some 15 million Model T's have poured out of Ford factories. The efficiency of Ford's manufacturing approach also allows him to continually reduce the price of his cars, from $780 in 1910 to $360 in 1916 to $290 in 1924.

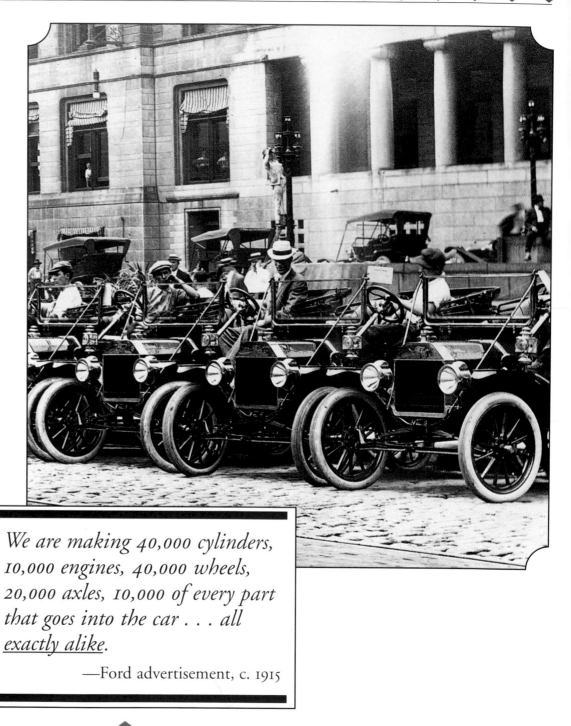

We are making 40,000 cylinders, 10,000 engines, 40,000 wheels, 20,000 axles, 10,000 of every part that goes into the car . . . all <u>exactly alike</u>.

—Ford advertisement, c. 1915

The low price of the Model T and of later models that Ford develops makes the automobile available to even the modest wage earner. But learning to drive the vehicles and keeping them in repair are other matters. America's roads, not built for cars, remain primitive until well into the 1930's, and accidents and breakdowns are common.

Perhaps the time will come when horses will be educated to the point where they will not be afraid of automobiles; but I doubt that for I have not seen the time yet that I was not afraid of them.

—Newspaper editor, 1911

Despite its hazards, the automobile is more quickly embraced than any other previous invention, and within a few years of its introduction it changes habits everywhere. Young men and women hoping to spend some time alone find the automobile the perfect vehicle in which to carry out their courtship. City dwellers make Sunday drive in the country a family ritual, while towns and cities become much more accessible to those who live in the country. Journeys to amusement parks, beaches and other recreation areas become easier than ever before. But for most car owners, just a trip anywhere in their own automobile is in itself a great form of entertainment.

The New York to St. Louis Automobile Parade, Louisiana Purchase Exposition.   Copyright 1904 by C. H. Graves.

Automobile at rim of the Grand Canyon

By the 1920's the automobile is regarded by countless American citizens as an absolute necessity, its ownership part of the American dream. "I'll go without food before I'll see us give up the car," exclaims one woman. "I'd rather do without clothes than give up the car," states another. And one 1920's housewife, when asked why her family maintains an automobile when it owns no bathtub, replies, "Why, you can't go to town in a bathtub."

> *Why on earth do you need to study what's changing this country? I can tell you what's happening in just four letters: A-U-T-O.*
>
> —From the book *Middletown*, by Robert and Helen Lynd, 1929

The invention of the automobile leads to the establishment of dozens of new businesses, such as tire companies, gas stations, repair garages and motels. It leads also to a brand-new pastime—automobile racing.

INDIANAPOLIS MOTOR SPEEDWAY
GREATEST RACE COURSE IN THE WORLD

Management
C.G. FISHER   F.H. WHEELER
A.C. NEWBY   J.A. ALLISON

For Americans, who have always been in love with speed and daring, automobile racing is the perfect sport. Racecourses, appropriately named speedways, are built throughout the nation, attracting millions of spectators, who cheer wildly for their favorite cars and drivers.

As the automobile captures American minds and hearts, once again there are those who are convinced that it is the most dramatic transportation device the world will ever know. The impact of the automobile gives them good reason for this belief, but like others before them, they still have not gauged the full extent of American ingenuity.

VISIONS OF FLIGHT

"I sometimes think," an early flying enthusiast states, "that the desire to fly is an ideal handed down to us by our ancestors, who in their grueling travels in prehistoric times, looked enviously on the birds soaring freely through space, at full speed, above all obstacles on the infinite highway of the air." For hundreds of years the possibility of human-controlled flight had been the subject of fond dreams and artists' imaginings.

In the 1800's, in the wake of so many successful inventions and the progress made with so many mechanical devices, efforts to take to the sky flourish. Many of these attempts at flight are conducted by men whose courage and ambition exceed their understanding of what it takes to launch men and women successfully into the heavens.

May not our mechanicians . . . be ultimately forced to admit that aerial flight is one of that great class of problems with which man can never cope, and give up all attempts to grapple with it?

—Noted astronomer Simon Newcomb, 1903

But by the 1890's there are men like Felix DuTemple and Clement Ader in France, Sir Hiram Maxim in England, Otto Lilienthal in Germany and Samuel Langley in the United States who, through experiments with balloons, wind tunnels and gliders, push humankind to the height of aeronautical success.

Wright brothers' first flight

> *Damned if they ain't flew [sic].*
>
> —Eyewitness to Wright brothers' first flight, December 17, 1903

Samuel Langley's flight attempt

The failed attempts of early aeronautical pioneers bring jeers and laughter from onlookers. But on December 17, 1903, two bicycle makers from Dayton, Ohio, brothers Orville and Wilbur Wright, stun the world. At 10:35 A.M., on the sands of Kitty Hawk, North Carolina, Orville controls their primitive airplane as it rises into the air, flies against the wind for 12 seconds, and lands 120 feet from the spot from which it was launched. It is the first flight in history in which a machine carrying a man has raised itself by its own power, flown under control and landed at an elevation as high as its point of departure.

THE DAYTON JOURNAL.

ORVILLE WRIGHT CONQUERS
AIR IN AMAZING FLIGHT

Years of Scientific Research Crowned
by Dayton Man in Record-
Breaking Test.

FLYING IS NOW CONCEDED
AS AN ESTABLISHED FACT

Cruises in Invisible Currents of Ether Now a
Certainty and Darius Green's Dream
Is Made a Living Reality.

Orville Wright a volé hier
pendant presque une heure

TOUS LES RECORDS D'AVIATION SONT BATTUS

To prove that their achievement is no fluke, the Wright brothers, with Wilbur as pilot, make three more successful flights on that same day, the longest being 852 feet in 59 seconds. In the years ahead the brothers will push aviation forward with other historic flights, including the successful trial in 1909 of a plane carrying a pilot and passenger 125 miles at a speed of 40 miles per hour. Like the great inventors Morse, Edison and Bell before them, the Wright brothers join the ranks of America's most honored heroes.

Although the Wright brothers' achievement at Kitty Hawk comes to be recognized as one of the milestones of history, the world is not immediately launched into the air age. Two years after their initial success, the Wrights remain the only persons to have achieved powered flight. But by 1910 brave pilots in the United States and abroad have taken to the air. Slowly but surely, the sight of the astounding new airborne machines, and of pilots, male and female, preparing to launch themselves into the skies, becomes less shocking.

> *Men cheered on and on as though there would be no end. And right then and there every man, woman and child of the multitude wanted to fly—up in the blue, cut away from the earth—fly—fly—oh, the ravishing delight of it.*
>
> —Spectator at early air meet, 1910

I ronically, the popularity of flying is most effectively pushed forward not by serious aeronautical innovators, but by daring early pilots and daredevils who capture the public's attention through the stunts they perform and the feats they accomplish. At county fairs and on barnstorming tours, they provide airplane rides at ten dollars for ten minutes and introduce men, women and children throughout the nation to the possibilities and thrills of flight.

JOIN THE
AIR SERVICE
and
SERVE
in
FRANCE

DO IT
NOW

J. Paul Verrees
1917

Some believe that the greatest role of the airplane will be as a weapon of war. In 1914 that theory is put to the test as World War I erupts in Europe. During the first three years of the war, German and British aircraft compete for rule of the skies. Almost immediately after the United States joins the fray in 1917, its military leaders become aware of the powerful impact that airplanes are having through ground strafing, artillery spotting and troop support. An intense effort is launched to build planes and a military air service, and by 1918 there are 740 American combat aircraft and almost 800 pilots.

The aerial accomplishments realized during World War I inspire further technological advances, and less than a year after the conflict ends, a regular airmail route is established between New York and Chicago. But like the Wright brothers' initial flight, it is a single event that most dramatically advances the future of aviation. In May 1927, a twenty-five-year-old aviator named Charles Lindbergh, competing for a $25,000 prize, takes off from a small airport on Long Island, New York. He is heading for Paris, striving to become the first person to fly nonstop across the Atlantic alone.

> *Our messenger of peace and goodwill has broken down another barrier of time and space.*
>
> —President Calvin Coolidge, 1927

For balance, Lindbergh carries all the gasoline that can be packed aboard his tiny plane, the *Spirit of St. Louis,* in a cased-in cockpit up front. He is literally flying blind. Thirty-three and a half hours later, after battling wind currents, fatigue and doubts about his precise whereabouts, he lands at his intended destination, Le Bourget airfield, outside Paris. A hundred thousand wildly cheering Frenchmen illuminate the airfield with their automobile headlights to aid the young flyer's night landing, greet him and carry him from his cockpit. When Lindbergh arrives back in America, he is given the greatest hero's welcome the nation has ever seen. The extraordinary attention his flight achieves sets the stage for the development of commercial aviation, an industry that blossoms in the 1930's.

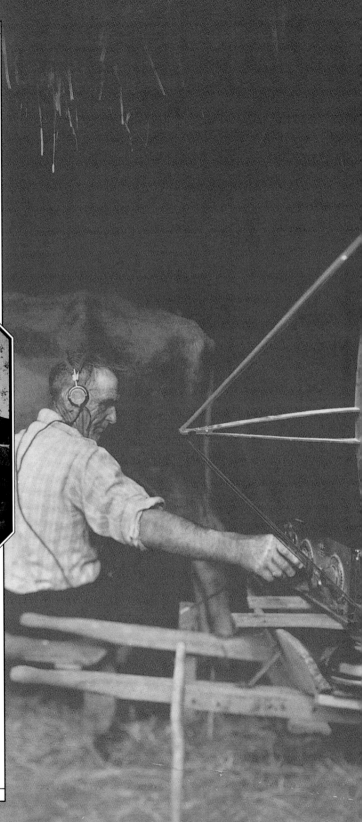

OTHER MARVELS

y 1930 Americans are now traveling the country by trolley, by train, in their own automobiles and, in increasing numbers, by air. The telegraph, the telephone, the typewriter and other new means of communication place them in touch with one another as never before. And 29 million families are being entertained by yet another marvel of invention: the radio.

he two men most responsible for developing the technology that makes radio possible are its separate inventors, the Italian Guglielmo Marconi and the American Dr. Lee De Forest. But it is a Russian immigrant, David Sarnoff, who makes radio an entertainment and information giant. In the 1920's Sarnoff establishes the nation's first broadcasting network, bringing music, news and regularly scheduled comedy and dramatic programs into both urban and rural homes.

E ven more dramatic than the impact of the radio is the phenomenon of motion pictures. By the 1920's Thomas Edison's early vision of the movies as a prime form of entertainment has been fully realized. By the end of the 1930's more than 85 million viewers a week flock to movie palaces in the cities and to small theaters across America.

Based on the SUPERMAN adventure feature appearing in SUPERMAN and ACTION COMICS magazines and in daily and Sunday newspapers coast to coast. Adapted from the SUPERMAN radio program.

with
SUPERMAN
KIRK ALYN · LYLE TALBOT
NOEL NEILL · TOMMY BOND

CHAPTER 6
ATOM MAN'S CHALLENGE

A COLUMBIA SERIAL

Screen Play by GEORGE H. PLYMPTON, JOSEPH F. POLAND and DAVID MATHEWS · Directed by SPENCER BENNET · Produced by SAM KATZMAN

The movies become so popular that they profoundly influence people's ideas and attitudes. The age of the celebrity is born, as movie stars like Charlie Chaplin, Rudolph Valentino, Lillian Gish and Greta Garbo become more famous than the nation's leaders. Movie producers, realizing the importance of attracting young viewers, create weekly, ongoing adventures called serials, and the Saturday matinee becomes an American institution.

The American inventive spirit not only improves the nation's standard of living, making it the highest in the world, but makes change through invention almost commonplace. The evidence that the inventive spirit is still very much alive is all around us today. The typewriter and the telegraph have been replaced in great measure by the computer and the fax machine. Picture taking and air travel have been revolutionized by instant photography and jet aircraft. Videocassettes now bring movies into the home, and television has become the world's most popular medium of entertainment.

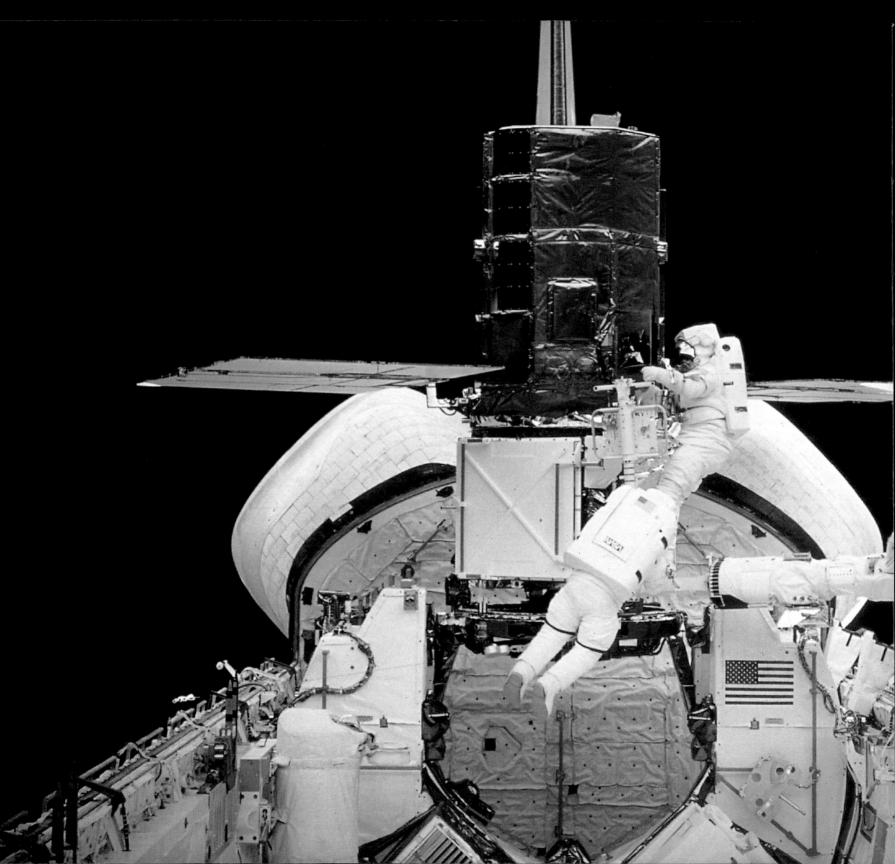

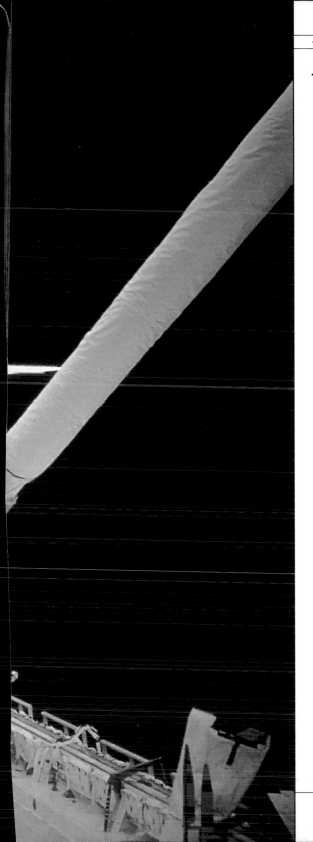

We have ventured into space and reached for the farthest stars. From our earliest inventions to our most recent, we have learned a most important lesson—almost nothing is impossible, and our dreams and horizons are limited only by our imaginations.

> *A lot of people ask . . . why a man is willing to risk. . . . Well, we've got to do it. We're going into an age of exploration that will be bigger than anything the world has ever seen. . . . If a man faces up to the [unknown] and takes the dare of the future, he can have some control over his destiny.*
>
> —Astronaut John Glenn, 1961

Photo courtesy of NASA

The Library of Congress

ll of the photographs, lithographs, engravings, paintings, line drawings, posters, song lyrics, song-sheet covers, broadsides and other illustrative materials contained in this book, with the exception of the photograph on pages 86 and 87, which comes courtesy of the National Aeronautics and Space Administration, have been culled from the collections of the Library of Congress. The Library houses the largest collection of stored knowledge on earth. Within its walls lie treasures that show us how much more than a "library" a great library can be.

The statistics that help define the Library are truly amazing. It has more books from America and England than anywhere else, yet barely one half of its collections are in English. It contains more maps, globes, charts and atlases than any other place on earth. It houses one of the largest collections of photographs in the world, the largest collection of films in America, almost every phonograph record ever made in the United States and the collections of the American Folklife Center. The Library also contains over six million volumes on hard sciences and applied technology.

It is a very modern institution as well. Dr. James Billington, the Librarian of Congress, has defined the Library's future through his vision of a "library without walls." "I see the Library of Congress in the future," he has said, "as an active catalyst for civilization, not just a passive mausoleum of cultural accomplishments of the past." A good example of this commitment is the Library's National Demonstration Laboratory, which, through hands-on work stations, offers over 200 examples of the latest innovations in interactive video and computer learning.

The Library of Congress was originally established to serve the members of Congress. Over the years it has evolved into a great national library. Unlike almost every other national library in the world, the Library of Congress does not limit the use of its collections to accredited scholars. Ours is a national library made by the people for the people, and is open to all the people. Fondly referred to as "the storehouse of the national memory," it is truly one of our proudest and most important possessions.

Index

Numbers in *italics* indicate photographs and illustrations.